SHIPPING STORAGE CONTAINER HOMES

FOR BEGINNERS

An Introductory Guide The Pros And Cons Of DIY Building An Eco-Friendly, Cargo, Storage House That's Robust, Safe, Durable, Cost-Effective, And Customizable For Off-Grid Living

Practical Guidebook

Stirling De Cruz Coleridge

Table of Contents

Introduction

My mission in this guidebook for beginners is to inspire, motivate and educate people to change their environment by using resources around them. But, it is vital to be aware of both *disadvantages and advantages* concerning storage container homes.

Please feel free to provide your feedback after reading this book or like and share.

We have a Facebook Group you can also join named: *storage container homes*.

@storagecontainerhomes

You will find information, plans, etc. on building your shipping container home. Please take a look, like and share our FB Page.

Shipping Cargo Storage Container Homes

If you've been thinking about building a storage container house, now is the time to jump on board with this adaptable and cost-effective construction option.

This section will present you with some useful suggestions for beginners and those just starting with their storage container journey.

Simply put, a storage container home is an entire house built using one or more containers—from manufactured ones like those used in shipping and construction to recycled paint buckets or surplus military bunkers.

If you haven't heard much about the storage container home, it's no wonder. But unfortunately, their popularity has generally been limited to off-grid and prepper lifestyles.

But that's starting to change.

They're ideal for building in areas that are prone to flooding or severe weather, as well as remote locations with little or no access to utilities such as water and electricity. However, some have stressed out about being so far from any neighbours or utilities will choose for themselves.

But as society becomes more environmentally conscious and the demand for affordable housing grows, the storage container home is becoming a widely discussed alternative to traditional construction methods.

And they're more popular than you might think. Since 2011, sales of these containers have increased by at least 15 per cent each year. And that's just in the US Overseas, the demand for these containers is equally as high.

For those interested in working with a storage container company, you'll want to keep all of this in mind. It's why we wrote this short article to provide you with some helpful tips for beginners.

But for now, let's take a look at what it takes to build your storage container home!

Here the top 5 things to know if you're new to DIY storage container construction:

1. **Size Matters**:

The single most important thing you need to know about your container home is the average size of the container. You wouldn't put a size ten foot in a size seven shoe. It just wouldn't fit. And that's why you need to make sure that the container you choose is large enough for your needs before you sign on the dotted line.

If it's not, then it doesn't matter how much you love your new home—you aren't going to be able to build it there.

2. **Constructing the Foundation**:

This one is just common sense. Without foundation, your storage container home will not have a home. So make sure you have a solid foundation before you start building your home.

That said, if you have access to solid soil and a good soil slope, then you're already good to go for up to two containers. If not, don't worry about it— you can still build an ideal container home as long as you keep things in perspective.

14

3. How to Build the Foundation:

Again, this is just common sense, but the more you know about building your storage container home materials, the easier it'll be to get a good foundation! For example, if you're building a container home out of concrete blocks or precast concrete slabs, it's best to make it on a solid basement base. Then, you can add additional footings for support underneath your container after it's up.

You can use sandbags to fill the holes from your foundation to help compensate for the uneven ground for other containers.

4. How to Build the Walls:

The walls of your container home are where you'll spend the most time and money. Sure, it might be cold out when you're trying to get started, but building them correctly will affect everything that comes later in life.

You need to make sure that your walls are strong enough to withstand the harsh weather and cold temperatures. If you don't, then your insulation is going to be useless. And that's one of the scariest things about building a new home from scratch.

But if you make sure that your walls are solid and sound, then you can expect them to last for years without any problems.

5. **How to Build the Roof**:

When building a roof on your storage container home, you don't need to be the best at carpentry. All you need to do is make sure that you have enough materials around. And at least one of them should be a tarp or plastic sheeting.

To make your life easier, you can also use chicken wire to help keep the cold out. But most importantly, the roof needs to be strong enough to withstand the harsh weather.

And that's it! Now that you've learned all of the basics, you're ready to go out and build your new home. But keep in mind that there's a lot more to building a house than just reading a few books!

So if you want to create your own storage container home, make sure that you use suitable, robust materials.

For example, corrugated steel containers used for solid foundations and other structures. As a bonus, they're entirely recyclable! That means that you'll be able to use them again for something else later on if you ever have to move.

And if you're able to find locally sourced materials, then you'll be helping the local economy and saving yourself a lot of money. Make sure that you use the proper methods for installing them! Otherwise, bad weather will get in and ruin everything.

The same is true for wood. A good rule of thumb is to use pressure-treated wood for your frame structure, but don't use it for insulation or anything else other than framing out your home.

If you're looking for something with a little more style, you can also use stone, brick or even cement blocks if you know how to install them properly!

Remember that the essential part of building a new home is doing it right. Your container home will be with you for many years to come if you do. And that's why it's so important to do your research!

How to Build a DIY Storage Container Home for Beginners

Remember, no matter how many books you've read or YouTube videos you've seen, if you follow the information in this book, you'll be able to build a sturdy and durable home at some point in the future.

And that's why it's so important to do your research before you start building.

All of the information is part of the process; it's essential to know every step of the way!

When you're familiar with everything that goes on behind the scenes, then you'll be able to get your project done on time and within budget.

The Pros Of Shipping Container Homes

Pros of Shipping Container Homes:

- *These containers can store personal belongings, such as furniture and large appliances.*
- *They are designed for ease of transportation and portability.*
- *Many stacked two high to create an excellent building form.*
- *They are also solar-heated in winter! (where applicable)*
- *The environmental impact is minimal. They are generally constructed of recyclable materials, have low energy requirements and come with a 30-year residential warranty.*

According to the Energy Policy Act of 2005:

Deciding to build a new home with shipping containers can reduce your overall building costs.

With many shipping containers being idle in US ports due to trade imbalances, you can save 20-60 per cent of the cost of traditional materials while using steel painted and structurally sound.

The benefits are endless when choosing between a shipping container home or another type of home.

If you are looking at shipping containers as your solution, it is crucial to plan.

Finding suitable containers for your needs, using containers in new or renovated areas, and making sure home codes will allow you to use them are all essential areas to consider.

With the help of an architect and designer, these containers are used as homes or accessory buildings.

By taking the time and effort to research these shipping container homes, you can ensure that they will be spacious enough for all of your needs.

Shown to be installed in rugged or remote areas.

Shipping containers make an eco-friendly alternative to traditional construction methods, which is why designers and architects are using them to build contemporary buildings.

Remodelling a home in California:

Remodelling can often cost you up to 35 – 50% of the original home price.

Shipping container homes are perfect for people who do not want to spend that much money on remodelling but still want a modern home.

Made of durable and long-lasting materials, they are often energy-efficient and come with a 30-year warranty.

In addition to all these benefits, they cost less than traditional construction methods.

With the proper planning and execution, shipping container homes can be as comfortable as any home built with conventional methods.

To get started:

Contact an architect or designer so that you can discuss your remodelling ideas before you buy a shipping container.

Consider the area where you like to live.

Decide whether you want to live in a city, rural area or a suburb.

Research the space that you need to build.

Think about how many bedrooms and bathrooms you need.

The Cons Of Shipping Container Homes

Magnuson, a reputable author of *"Shipping Container Homes: An Introduction to Building with Containers,"* states:

A container is helpful for a temporary neighbourhood of homes.

The primary disadvantages are temporary housing and cannot be used everywhere.

The construction process is highly labour-intensive; thus, a labour shortage is likely. Therefore, using containers outside urban centres would create higher costs and inconveniences for the homeowners.

A container is also not a good choice for an extended period. The materials degrade, the foundations erode, and the structures become unsafe. However, the housing may be used to house homeless people temporarily.

The logistics of shipping containers are currently under severe pressure in many countries due to economic conditions and a shortage of building materials.

This would inevitably lead to a lack of resources for any other pre-planned uses, such as the building of container homes.

Many people believe that shipping containers are not suitable for long-term living. There are many reasons, from the poor insulation to the thin walls and floors. Because of this, there have been many experiments and new ways to use containers have been discovered.

Part of these experiments includes making shipping container homes.

Unfortunately, containers are not as durable as they seem.

However, containers are perfect for temporary housing, as they can be used in any climate and location.

Costs associated with conventional construction methods are expensive.

Shipping containers can make houses that cost much less than traditional houses, with the same features and quality.

Making an affordable house is a great challenge today due to the high costs of materials and construction methods.

This means that building a house from shipping containers could be an alternative, as it can be made at a relatively low cost.

The construction process for shipping container homes is also much less complicated than it would be with conventional housing.

Many resources are available for people looking to make their shipping container home.

There are many shipping container homes in different parts of the world.

These houses have a variety of styles, from modern to kitsch. Many of these are built as holiday homes or for people with money. This means that the people who live in these shipping container homes enjoy high standards and quality.

This is unlike any other developing country worldwide, where no one lives in a container home.

Over time, it will become more common to see shipping container homes and other valuable methods.

Shipping container homes are now a reality, and it is only a matter of time before more resources are available for individuals seeking to make them.

The cost of shipping container homes is gradually decreasing, so it will soon be affordable for more people.

Shipping containers can easily be reused if storms do not damage them.

They have been used to make homes, offices and restaurants. Not only that but they have recently been used as temporary prisons in many countries.

Hopefully, this trend will continue, so more people worldwide can live comfortably in shipping container homes.

Shipping container homes can be made into anything, as long as the materials are standard and the construction process is followed correctly.

These shipping container homes are built for families and businesses in urban areas.

They are a good, long term option for all families, especially those looking for low-cost housing.

Shipping container homes are made of steel and wood, making them durable and easy to maintain.

They also have lower energy costs and better insulation than traditional houses. In addition, these materials keep the house warm in the winter and cool in the summer.

Because containers can be reused, they are environmentally friendly. This is because they can be chopped up and put back together whenever necessary. Shipping containers are also very portable.

They are easy to move on and off the ships and store for future use.

Coupled with these features, shipping container homes provide better construction features than conventional houses with similar costs.

Using shipping container homes for housing is not just about the cost of living but also environmental concerns.

Shipping containers have a steel frame that is strong and durable. In addition, the walls and roof can be made from wood, sustainable material in itself.

The walls and roof can also be made from other sustainable materials, such as grass and straw. This means that more people will live in shipping container homes without worrying about hurting the environment.

Not only do shipping container homes help the environment, but they also help people in need of better housing.

Shipping containers are stackable, so it is easy to fit many into smaller spaces. In addition, the containers can be stacked as high as required for any given situation.

Are Shipping Container Homes Safe?

Backyard cabins made from shipping containers pop up around the United States in places where land is scarce, and building codes can be restrictive.

These structures – known as "micro-homes" or "shovel-ready homes" – are inexpensive to build, require little construction experience or permits, and operate on a proven design.

The cost of purchasing a pre-manufactured unit may be higher than owning a house with similar square footage, but they are less expensive than traditional home designs. And depending on how much work you are willing to do yourself, your costs can be even lower.

Homes built from used shipping containers are strong and free of lead-based paints. This is more than you can say for most houses built during the 1960s and 1970s.

The original containers these were constructed with were recycled military steel, which means the homes were produced under stricter guidelines than new construction.

Shipping containers are relatively easy to move around and are less likely to require permits than other housing types.

Homeowners can choose their locations and design their homes to be energy-efficient, weather-resistant and aesthetically appealing. They are made of steel, robust, durable and fire-resistant.

Shipping container homes are a viable housing option for people on a budget who want to live in a free house of lead paint or other harmful materials. For those interested in custom designs and having access to building plans, container home kits can be purchased from contractors who specialise in building this housing style.

Standard Size Of A Shipping Container Home

A shipping container's standard sizes and dimensions are 8ft wide, 8ft 6in high, and 20ft long.

This means a space above each container of approximately 10ft. Before modifications to the standard dimensions of a shipping container, it first needs to be transported on a flatbed truck.

Once onsite, crane removal and erection can commence. After the containers are stacked, a mezzanine floor can be installed between the two containers, providing up to 10ft of additional headroom.

After this, the container can be modified to include floorboards, new doors and windows and internal functions. This kitchen has a free-standing cooker and fridge/freezer.

The standard modular dimensions of each shipping container will allow for most houses on wheels to be built within the 8ft width.

However, if the floor area does not reach the required minimum of 20ft x 8ft, a fraction of this will have to be removed after the container has been installed.

Also, generally, only 12ft wide container spaces can be built onsite. However, the modular nature of shipping containers also allows adding extensions or additional container "wings" to the house.

These additions will also have to be constructed upon arrival at the site. If there are any structural changes, these will be made before an extension can be added.

Building Shipping Container Homes

The standard home is around 8' x 8' containers, accommodating two double-height living area rooms. Basement units are also available, and these can consist of a bedroom, bathroom, kitchen and living area.

These pre-designed houses have been designed by expert architects and are generally built using 8' x 8' containers.

They can be adapted to suit the needs of families, single men or women, designed with the flexibility to suit individual lifestyles.

They are designed with a minimum floor space of 20ft x 8ft to enable you to build an extension if they do not meet the requirements.

How Do You Insulate a Shipping Container Home?

Shipping container homes are a popular choice for do-it-yourself who want to build their own home, but there are some unique concerns about insulation.

For example, if the walls of your shipping container home will be exposed, you need to determine how you'll insulate them.

As with a metal building, radiant heat can cause condensation if you fail to insulate the walls of your shipping container home.

If the walls are exposed, you'll need to apply a layer of insulation to the outside of the walls.

You can apply either rigid foam insulation or spray-applied foam insulation to the walls. Both of these options have an R-value higher than traditional fibreglass batt insulation.

To reduce drafts and condensation, it's recommended that you also apply a vapour barrier between the insulation and exterior wall sheathing.

It's not necessary to insulate shipping container home floors in most regions.

However, if you choose to insulate container home floors, you can use concrete pavers or hydro-insulated floor tiles. Both of these options have R-values that are higher than typical hardwood flooring.

Install rigid insulation between the container home timbers and the floor joists. For example, if you're using a shipping container home with lumber framing, install 2x4 studs 16 inches apart in the corners and 2x4 studs over the centre of the room for added support for your shipping container house structure.

After installing the insulation, you can use plywood to build your floor.

A Roof To A Shipping Container Home

If you've purchased a shipping container for your home or storage, then you might have thought about covering it with a standard roof. This is doable and affordable if you aren't afraid to take on a little project.

However, as with any project involving power tools and construction, there are some things to consider and address so that the finished product will give you a look you want.

After spending hours online researching shipping container homes, I was amazed that there isn't much information on improving the outside appearance with easy DIY methods.

So what I will do is share with you what I have learned.

If you plan to make your shipping container home into a complete structure, you will need to add proper insulation and electrical to meet the building code for safety reasons.

It is not good to have an open container insulating from the outside since external weather elements will affect it.

You may have an option to add a metal roof, but if that isn't an option, you can create your own by purchasing inexpensive material from your local hardware store.

Materials Needed for Roofing Container Home

A solid adhesive such as tar or hot glue will hold the material in place and be used on all seams.

Rolling sod works very well and is available at most nurseries and home improvement stores.

If you have a wood deck in your container, you can use wood shingles to cover it. They come in round or square shapes, so I would match the shape of the roofing material to that of the shingles you are using.

The Exterior Walls

One thing that bugs me about shipping container homes is that they almost always require a layer of siding over the containers. The natural beauty of a container house is the plain, exposed nature of the container.

If you don't have access to siding and or windows, you will need to apply aluminium foil or some other material over the walls. The foil can be purchased at your local hardware store, and it works very well to cover windows and doors.

Windows

It's not a good idea to put windows in a shipping container home since they can break easily or become damaged by weather elements such as rain, wind and even hail.

If you plan to add windows to your container, you should consider putting in a glass wall with a door that will lead to an outside deck.

Consider using plexiglass so that the windows are protected from damage.

If you use plexiglass, make sure that they are tinted or at least use blackouts so that the sun isn't allowed in and help keep the interior cool.

All doors for the home should be made of natural wood so that the original structure is not compromised in any way.

So if you want to add a layer of insulation to your container home, you can do so using inexpensive materials.

Depending on where you live, you will need to make sure that the exterior of your container is insulated adequately so that it doesn't melt in the heat and crack in extreme cold weather conditions.

If the container is used for storage, you will want to consider an interior wall insulated with styrofoam and then covers the styrofoam with a layer of heat reflective material.

I hope that this section has given you some great ideas on how to improve your shipping container home.

Remember, it's YOUR dream, so build it and make it come true!

What US States Allow Shipping Container Homes?

In most United States, it is illegal to construct and live in a home built from shipping containers. However, permits are currently given out in California, Nevada and Washington.

This will begin to change, though, as more people get behind the idea and develop new ways to get around building codes regarding the use of shipping containers. The process is slow, but it's happening throughout US cities.

Planning For Your Shipping Container Home

If you're thinking about building a shipping container home, you'll want to check your local zoning laws. Some places do not allow for this type of building. If your community does allow for shipping container homes, you will have to set up a plan where everything goes and how it is all supposed to work together.

You will also have to figure out what type of foundation the home will need. A regular foundation is required for the house to be approved by city inspectors.

Still, you might be able to work around this requirement by having it look like someone built a regular foundation and then added the shipping containers onto it.

Some companies are making special foundations for shipping container homes, and you should contact one of these companies to see what they can do to help out.

The Legal Issues With Shipping Container Homes

To live in a shipping container home, you will have to get permits. However, if you are building one on your land and it is located far away from everyone else, you might be able to make it without anyone knowing.

This won't work well in city areas, though, and you must check your local laws and building codes before making any plans for one of these homes.

In some communities, zoning laws prohibit people from living in shipping container homes.

These laws are different from town to town, but in most cases, people who live in these areas can only live in them if they have permission from their neighbours.

Shipping Container Homes Are Not Suitable For Everyone

If you plan on living in a shipping container home, you will have to keep it clean and up to code. While it is easy to clean, some people are hard to live with, and you might have problems if you don't watch them.

Shipping Container Homes For The Disadvantaged

The conventional wisdom is to build these homes as cheaply as possible in the cheapest real estate and then sell them for profit. But what if these container homes were used for community use and not for profit?

For example, a community centre could have fifteen or twenty homes on five acres of land.

Also, there are many empty lots in our neighbourhoods where old industrial sites and warehouses used to stand.

These lots are often too small to construct traditional homes, and the land cost is prohibitive.

Psychologically, returning to our roots (container design) may be the only way to rebuild the community in our urban centres.

The concept of using shipping containers has been widely prevalent through community recycling initiatives, as a storehouse for community projects and outdoor activities.

With the growing popularity and alternative usage of shipping containers as a material to build buildings comes an interest to build cargo container homes, specifically as an affordable housing solution.

These homes are typically used for short-term accommodation in recreational and business contexts, such as a holiday cottage.

They are also used for migrant workers accommodation as a transitional dwelling before or after permanent housing is found.

They have also been used for low-cost student accommodation, with successful examples in Australia and the United Kingdom.

Shipping container homes are usually made from old, used containers. Purchasing new containers for this purpose can be expensive and is not always an option. In addition, shipping containers can be acquired at a fraction of the cost of a typical house.

Because they are cheap to purchase and ship, they offer homeowners the opportunity to build or remake an existing home with little outlay in either time or money.

In the United States, it is standard for these homes to be placed on platforms or stilts. This serves a double purpose because the ground area is not used for living space, and the house itself is elevated above ground level with access by stairs rather than a small set of stairs.

In this way, shipping container homes can provide the same security level as raised houses without redesigning foundation and floor plans.

The United Nations has developed procedures for the humanitarian use of old shipping containers. Many shipping companies donate their old containers to humanitarian agencies, used as housing in refugee camps, such as the UNHCR camps in Chad and Kenya.

They are also used by NGOs, including the International Medical Corps, World Vision, Mercy Corps, and Habitat for Humanity.

In Mexico, shipping containers are available as house kits. They are marketed to the lack of affordable housing and are considered the first industrialised nation in the Americas. In total, Mexico has 73 manufacturers who offer this product for sale.

While shipping container homes are often considered a means to reduce construction costs and save money, several issues may make this not worthwhile.

First of all, shipping containers themselves may be expensive to purchase. The fact that used or new ones are not affordable for most people means that this method of home building is only a viable option for those who can spend the money to dispose of shipping containers and then purchase new ones.

Secondly, shipping container homes may not be as attractive as traditional homes. This is precisely the case if they are built in an area surrounded by buildings made with more conventional materials.

In such communities, shipping containers might not be an attractive option in terms of appearance and may even appear to be unsafe.

Third, while they are often built by volunteers and community groups who already have experience with similar work, shipping container homes may not be made in record time.

For example, a typical height of a shipping container is eight feet.

Therefore, building sites where eight-foot-tall containers are used tend to take longer and require more skill than sites where taller buildings are constructed, especially if foundations need to be dug.

Fourth, while shipping container homes have been used successfully to solve housing shortages in many locations worldwide, they have not been widely employed to solve the housing problem in the United States since they are not sufficiently cheap.

In the United States, shipping container homes are built by volunteers and are cheaper if purchased new rather than disposed of for free. However, the high cost of a single container means that this method is only financially viable for small projects.

In the United States, container homes are typically used to construct temporary or permanent housing.

However, it is possible to build a container home that complies with building codes and can be used as a permanent residence, such as the ships-based student accommodation at the University of Greenwich in London (pictured above).

The chief advantage of using shipping containers is that they are used widely in the global shipping trade, which means they are virtually indestructible and moveable.

This makes it possible to attain quality construction without spending much money. In addition, shipping containers can be built in record time and offer security at the same level as a raised house.

Cost Of Shipping Container Homes

Whether you're looking for a shipping container home for sale or to buy a home that's been built using these containers, here are some prices regarding the shipping container homes in the market today.

Price: A low cost-per-square-foot average is around $10–$15/sq. Ft.

Price: Higher quality at $40-$60/sq. Ft.

Price: Custom-built container homes from $100 - $200/sq. ft.

These prices may differ from State to State and change over time.

Shipping Container Homes Advantages

They are relatively energy efficient, typically achieving insulation and R-values with conventional home construction.

They have a very high recycling rate – each square foot of a shipping container can be recycled into another one.

Shipping containers are less susceptible to wind and earthquakes than conventional modular homes with sturdy construction, often built with wood frames.

Shipping Container Homes Disadvantages

Shipping containers have a meagre thermal value. Consequently, they are less comfortable in hot and cold climates. In addition, they are not as durable as traditional homes.

Due to their lightweight tend to be unstable in stormy weather, especially with large waves in the water. Free-standing shipping container homes are also prone to flooding during heavy rains or flooding due to high tides.

Do Shipping Container Homes, Last Long?

The Onsite storage container homes in Singapore are trendy among Singaporeans because they cater to the housing needs of most ordinary people here.

Most families are clear that the ultimate goal of a housing unit is to provide shelter and peace of mind. The onsite storage container homes in Singapore, as well as overseas, deliver these goals very well.

However, most people do not know that they have more life left than expected.

The life expectancy of a shipping container is 20 to 30 years of use which means that the housing containers can still be used and rented out long after the initial duration they were built in.

Compared to other building materials such as wood, concrete, steel and glass, which usually last for a shorter period than their projected product duration, shipping container homes hold their value very well.

Another advantage of these housing units is that these units allow people with minimal budgets to own an efficient and comfortable home.

The shipping container homes in Singapore and overseas are made from steel, a material that can be recycled in many ways.

This is why most people agree that the price of these shipping container houses is higher than its actual value.

Types Of Shipping Container Homes In Singapore

There are many various designs and kinds of shipping container homes that you may build, but they all have one thing in common: you will use 20-foot sea containers as the foundation of your home.

This building will be constructed in a factory and then shipped to your land. This design is very economical because the construction team only has to worry about your home's foundation and structural stability.

The rest of the work can quickly be done with specialised tools plus modern technology today.

If you want to know more about these types of shipping container homes.

The Advantages of Using Shipping Container Homes

You should know many things about these types of container homes, but the benefits that you can get from using these products for your own home outweigh all the disadvantages.

The shipping container homes will cost less because you will use recycled materials for all the processes needed to create this type of building.

Building houses out of recycled materials is a modern trend, and it will allow everyone to enjoy cheap housing units at an even lower price.

Shipping Container Home Rust

People often ask, "*Does Shipping Container Home Rust*?"

Shipping container homes have been the rage for quite some time, especially among those concerned about their earth-friendly, affordable and affordable-to-build nature. And it's not just a matter of "if" they will rust - it's a matter of "when".

Rust is one of the crucial things that container homes will have to deal with.

It's important to understand that the containers aren't going to last forever, so you have to take steps to ensure that they will last as long as possible and be safe for you, your family and your precious belongings.

They were adequately Assembling Your Shipping Container Home or Commercial Building "The Right Way".

Although they are inherently structurally sound, shipping containers are sometimes not assembled correctly from the factory - this can lead to a whole host of problems down the road.

So, you must assemble these containers as best as possible.

The Bottom Line

If you own a shipping container and are interested in turning it into a permanent home or commercial building, don't just assemble it onto your property.

Instead, be sure to get professional help from someone like a Shipping Container Building Company to ensure that you get your container home built correctly.

Shipping Container Homes Hold Value

Daren Bader is an engineer and a software systems analyst by trade, but he's been dabbling in housing market for the past six years.

Discovered a way to build homes out of used shipping containers, and [he's] developed plans for a shipping container home that he says can be created for $30,000-$40,000."

This is less than half the cost of some other prefabricated homes on the market. Bader is also confident that the homes will hold their value since shipping containers have historically risen 18.6% per year since 2000.

Bader says, "If you look [at] the resale value of these things, typically you get about a 20 per cent return on your investment in about three years."

But Bader isn't the only one to notice this trend. Homebuyers and builders in the UK are rushing to buy used shipping containers.

For example, one British company has built a single-story house out of 23 steel containers.

One of the company's founders says, "Steel is a material that tends to go up in price each year, and so it costs us about $30,000 to make a house from shipping containers."

This is comparable to the cost of other prefabricated houses.

Homebuyers in the UK pay $29,000 for homemade from steel shipping containers.

But these homes don't come cheap.

The company's structure cost $100,000 to build, making their shipping container houses the most expensive ones on the market. But you can also buy an eight-person home for about $75,000 in the US.

A company in Colorado built a home for about $15,000 using 400 used shipping containers.

Then there's the genuinely crazy option of building your own home. But, again, there are numerous resources online if you want to learn how to create your own.

Shipping Container Homes Predictable Costs

Firstly, you have to recognise that Container Homes have a significant upfront cost in materials.

Here is a chart showing the material costs for, say, a house built with six wall panels:

The savings offset the cost in time and labour. For example, one person can build up 36-48 ft. on site, 8 hours per day (*6 days per week*) and that person will have a significant profit over their switch time and labour costs.

The math is elementary: savings versus costs:

(36 ft. high X 8 ft. long X 8 ft. wide) = 288 sq. ft.

2x4 X .90 = 2,688 board feet per container (Hence board over cost is $5760.)

The roofing cost is $7000.

Subtract roofing materials from total labour costs: ($5760 - $7000) / 288 sq. feet = $20.

So, the labour cost overtime is $5,240.00 (8 hours per day x 6 days per week), and the project profit is $2,880.00.

The math also shows that you need three containers to build a house that size, and each container costs $40,000 (for materials).

It should be noted that this is for a house size of only 36 ft. high X 48 ft. long by eight ft. wide (288 sq. ft.)

This is NOT a shipping container modular homemade from multiple containers.

Shipping Container Homes Can Be Built In A Day? ~ NOT!

Another common misconception is that Container homes can be built in a day because the steel frame is so easy to assemble and install.

But, these are not stick-built houses, so you need to prepare the site and set them in place.

For example, wet concrete is poured into buckets placed on the floor and wall columns. Also, the Container Homes need to be prepared for the foundation and electrical work.

It can take around a week at the very least to build one of these container homes from scratch.

However, it should also be noted that at least one of the individuals who have some experience with steel framing know how to use leverage properly.

This shows that most people do not have this kind of experience. But there are plenty of people who can handle any number of projects.

Shipping Container Homes
No Low Initial Cost

This one infuriates me. The initial cost for a house-made from these containers is about $35,000, including the 2, 6' high walls and site preparation. (*The $5,500 per container cost does not include the steel foundation framing and fasteners.*)

So let's review:

Building an elevated steel frame [36 ft. high X 48 ft. long X 8 ft. wide] with wood, steel, and fasteners will cost $5,500.

Which would you rather have, a stick-built house with columns and beams set upon a foundation or a container home? (In the first case, a builder could charge $20-25 per sq., ft.

In the second, they would need to be set on a foundation and charged $10-15 per sq. ft.)

A shipping container home is also going to have steel framing. So what do you think you will do differently when the time comes to add on a house addition or kitchen?

You will have to start over with basic framing techniques, which means more equipment and materials and most likely a more significant price tag.

Do You Need A Steel Foundation For A Shipping Container Home?

Shipping Container Homes are shipped to the site, moved into place and frame built. They are not like traditional stick-built structures where a foundation is created first, then the home is built upon it. So, let's look at a more rational set of materials:

2x6 x 8 thick studs wall X 8' tall T1-11 floor panel X 1" wood subfloor X 12 ft.

high extension 1" sheetrock X 12 ft. high extension

2x6 floor joist X 16' long T1-11 roof panel X 30 year shingles 2x6 rafter and ridge board X 16' long 2x4 floor framing X 48' long

Some of the cheaper steel home units have decks, but most do not. So, you need to know that a 30' high wall needs a truss system and a decent foundation. That is a project that should not be taken lightly.

These systems usually run around $6,000 out of pocket, in cash. And add another $7,000 for the shipping containers.

So, we are looking at an extra $13,000 or so just to build the foundation and frame the structure. So you really should think twice about where you will place these things. If it's not a good

location, then you might as well forget
it.

Shipping Container Home Warranty

This is one of the most amazing facts: they have a 30-year warranty on their homes. I'm lost for words. Think about how many things you don't have a warranty on:

car parts, craftwork, kitchen appliances, furniture, and so on.

Some buildings and houses do not give warranties anymore because the elements are so difficult to control nowadays.

The shipping container home warranty is unheard of, something I have never seen before in my entire life.

Tiny House v Storage Container Home

What is the difference between a storage container home and a tiny house? They are the same at the end of the day.

The difference is that tiny house enthusiast are more likely to use a storage container as their primary home base.

In contrast, others use it as a temporary home until they can build or purchase a permanent residence.

Storage container homes have become popular among millennials and after foreclosure because they offer an affordable option for those just getting out of college who need to move into their first place quickly.

Storage containers are also easy to customise and install, making them flexible structures that accommodate any desired lifestyle.

Storage containers provide a great alternative to traditional homes, especially in urban areas where space is of the essence. They can be customised to fit basic needs or modified to create a luxurious home.

Storage container homes are the same as any standard house because they offer the same living and working environments. The only difference is that these units are built using cargo containers converted into homes.

These storage container homes come in many different sizes and styles, depending on your requirements and budget.

Most people get their containers in the form of a kit. This means that the container has already been converted, and all you have to do is your

96

customisation work. Apart from being cost-effective, shipping containers offer other benefits, including:

Affordability

When you want to build a house, you need to consider many factors, including the location, materials used and size of the property.

This means that building a home can be expensive, depending on where you are located. However, shipping containers are an affordable option for those looking for budget-friendly homes.

Durability

Shipping containers are made from steel which is a strong material. This means that shipping containers will not easily get damaged or destroyed by harsh weather elements such as high winds, hurricanes and tornadoes. Even if the hull of the container is damaged, its insides remain safe.

However, you should ensure that your container has been adequately prepared before using it as a home.

You can also ensure durability by purchasing a new shipping container rather than a second-hand one.

They are easy to maintain

Shipping containers can be used daily, and they do not require much maintenance. The only time you need to do some maintenance work is when you want to change the interior design or exterior of the shipping container.

Also, if you live in a warm area, storage containers help keep your home cool and comfortable because they provide shade below.

These containers are also fire and rodent-proof, which means that they will serve you for many years before getting another one.

Shipping Containers are durable.

Storage containers offer incredible resistance to various weather elements such as sun and storm.

They can also withstand high winds, hurricanes and other natural disasters. For example, while many homes are destroyed during a hurricane or storm, people living in a shipping container home can stay safe.

The insulation and design of these containers ensure that you remain comfortable at all times.

You will not experience any change in temperature during the winter or summer seasons because storage containers retain heat or cold depending on the conditions outside.

Energy efficiency

Shipping containers are energy-efficient. While on the go, shipping containers are made from steel which is an energy-efficient material.

They help save energy because you cannot use lots of electricity to heat and cool this temporary home.

It also helps save on heating costs because shipping containers do not require extensive heating during wintertime and summertime months.

Studies have shown that shipping container homes can provide up to an 80% reduction in your energy bills.

They are easily accessible to the public.

Most homes are not suitable for shipping container homes because you need to have a medium and high level of expertise to install these structures. Usually, people wait for years before deciding to build their own homes.

A storage container home can be an excellent option for those who need a quick and inexpensive home.

Shipping container homes are easy to find online, especially on different construction sites. You will find that most people construct their first shipping containers where they live today.

In conclusion, you can find shipping container homes online if you search for them. However, they are typically found in different locations, such as construction and storage sites.

You will find them in a container shop with one room, two rooms and more inside. However, if you are looking for a freight container home that can be used as your permanent home, there are more options to consider when choosing the perfect design for your home.

This means that you have to assess your financial situation and lifestyle to get the perfect home for your needs.

It's important to consider all types of containers available before making a final decision. Shipping container homes are the best option for people who need cheap home options that are easy to design and maintain.

They are perfect for rural areas where they can be used as guest houses, storage units or even converted into buildings like libraries, restaurants and more.

In addition, they are an eco-friendly alternative for those looking for a way to design their homes cheaply, quickly and easily.

Before you decide to purchase a shipping container home, you should ensure that the following factors are considered:

Size of the container:

It would help if you looked at the size of the container to ensure that it will be big enough to accommodate your belongings.

While you may be familiar with the measurements of your home, you must get a container big enough to fit all your possessions.

This will make it much easier for you to move from one location to another when required. If you like the design, you can consider customising it to fit in with your preferences and needs.

Features:

Shipping container homes have a lot of features that you can choose from. Some of these features include but are not limited to:

- Choose the best location for your storage container home. When you purchase a shipping container home, you must make sure that the closest place is possible that is convenient and affordable so that you do not have to travel too far when moving house.

The frame's design should be appropriate for your preferences and needs. It would help if you got a container home with an attractive design always to look beautiful.

If you want to modify the structure, you can buy a pre-modification kit to change your mind and make any necessary changes quickly.

- A shipping container should have enough storage space inside for all your belongings. You should also be able to add additional storage space if necessary or only if it is available in the design of the container.

- You can get a container home that is simple in design so that you do not have to spend a lot of time working on it.

These shipping containers are easy to build, and they are also highly customisable. Therefore, you do not need to go through a difficult period of designing if you decide to buy one.

- The container should be easily accessible for people who need the materials for the project or who want to start the project. Therefore, you should ensure that all of your materials are in the right place and easy to access.

- You should make sure that the design of the container home is suited to your needs.

- The container home should have a high level of insulation so that the temperature inside remains constant all year round. This will help save you money when heating your home during wintertime or cooling down during summertime.

- It should be easy to construct the shipping container home.

If you are looking for a quick and easy way to build your own home, then look for one that is easy to assemble when it arrives. It should be possible to get started on building your new house immediately after the purchase.

- The shipping container home should have a warranty covering all the materials used on the construction.

109

This will help ensure that the container you have purchased is good quality and can last long. It will also help protect you from any costs involved in making repairs or replacements.

- It should be possible to transport the shipping container home when needed. If you purchase a container at home, you may need to move it from one place to another if necessary. It would help if you looked for transportation details that are clearly outlined when you buy it.

- The container should have all the necessary building materials to assemble the home.

When you buy a shipping container home, make sure it comes with all the necessary items for construction and no additional purchases are required.

- There are different types of containers available depending on your preferences and needs. For example, you can choose a mobile container transported from one place to another, a permanent constructed storage unit or anything in between.

It's important to consider all available options before making a final decision.

- You should check the containers for any damages before purchasing them or signing a contract. This will help avoid adding costs when problems are identified with the boat container you want to buy or rent.

It helps to have this done by an independent inspector so you can get an impartial review of any damage on the boat container.

- All containers will have a set of information printed on the outside that you need to look out for. In some cases, you will find the exact measurements of

the container, and you can compare it to your current home.

This helps make sure that everything fits perfectly when it arrives, and there is no need for any modification or change in design.

- You should make sure that all of your details are correct when you fill up the paperwork for purchasing a shipping container home. This will help avoid any added costs or delays.

-Getting a shipping container home is simple.

All you need to do is select one you like from the different options available and sign up for the shipping container home service.

You can then either pay for it with a deposit and wait for the container to be delivered, or you can already start building your house from the actual delivery of the container home.

Make sure that the legal details are signed before going ahead with your purchase. In addition, you should make sure that you understand all the terms and conditions before agreeing to any purchase.

Once your storage container home arrives at your doorstep, it is ready to start construction. The shipping container homes are usually delivered fully assembled, so there are no complications involved in construction. This makes it very simple for storage container owners to start the building process.

If you are looking for high-quality construction services, you should consider using a professional contractor or manufacturer for all your building requirements.

It will benefit you if you are looking for one that offers the best quality services and has all the necessary qualifications and experience to help you out. In addition, you will be glad that you decided to use these professionals if things go wrong during the construction process.

You should choose a company that provides all the services you will need during construction, which includes:

- Custom design and layout of your building plan.

- Assistance with the building code aspects for your home.

This would be important if you plan to get a permit for your home. This is usually done before you even begin construction. You must ensure that all required permit requirements are met before starting your project.

This can be done by getting a detailed drawing of your building plan and getting the assistance of a professionally registered architect.

- The essential construction services.

This is usually done by certified builders, carpenters, plumbers, etc. They will assist in the construction project, including plumbing, electric installations, painting, etc.

This would depend on the type of container home you buy, as some will provide these services while others may not. So, again, it is best to check with the manufacturer or provider before purchasing.

- Assistance with house design and layout.

This would be important for you if you plan to get a permit for your home. This is usually done before you begin construction, just like the first point stated above.

You can also get professional help from an architect or builder when getting the design plan for your home approved before the building begins.

- Assistance with getting permits and legal paperwork.

This is usually important if you plan to purchase a property and move into it instead of building on your land. In this case, you need to hire professionals who would assist you in getting everything approved.

You may also need to get a permit for building your container home, depending on the state where you live. Make sure that these details checked before purchasing your shipping container home.

It is better to look for a company that provides all these services. Then, you can choose your preferred company and make sure they are certified, registered and have the necessary experience to help you out.

You can check their credentials online or speak with other customers of theirs who have used them before. You will soon find out that many professional companies in the market provide excellent quality services to their clients.

If you decide to hire a professional, you should consider getting insurance coverage for your container home.

This is important to protect your investment just in case something goes wrong.

Many online resources are available, including articles and books to help you consider a container conversion.

In addition, online communities have many members who have gone through converting a shipping container into their homes, which can help you when investing in your own container home.

Container homes are usually more affordable than traditional houses, making them an attractive household option for many people.

They are also a good choice for people who want to invest in sustainable living as they can be made from recycled materials.

Maybe one of the most significant advantages of buying a shipping container home is its portability.

This makes them suitable for many different purposes, including a backyard studio, guest house or office.

They can even be used as recreational cabins on dense camping grounds when coupled with the necessary additions and upgrades.

The main reasons for their popularity are the unique design and minimal cost.

What Is Sustainable Living?

If you think it's something that involves gardening, rainwater collection systems, and some travel to exotic locations now and then, you're wrong!

There's nothing more sustainable than learning how to sustain yourself — whether that means spending less money, knowing where your food comes from, or just staying hydrated.

It is a revolutionary concept because the days of spending large amounts of money on things big corporations use are quickly coming to an end (*or at least should*).

1. SUSTAINABLE LIVING — BUT WHY?

First and foremost, it's essential to understand the difference between sustainable living and everyday living.

Everyday living means we're buying too much stuff from big corporations, and we're not in control of our own lives.

When we try to buy things that don't necessarily serve us, we invite corporations that make our clothes or food to keep putting profits before people.

These corporations are why our schools and hospitals run at over-budgeted costs and why our world is so polluted.

But when we live sustainably, it's not about living in a cave but instead about minimising our use of resources.

It means finding ways to reduce your environmental impact by using less water, less energy and fewer resources than you would in a normal lifestyle.

I'm not saying there's anything wrong with wanting big house or fancy clothes, but when you're spending so much money that you can't pay your bills because of it, has the cost been worth it?

2. SUSTAINABLE LIVING — WHY DO WE NEED TO DO IT?

There are only so many resources in the world, and they are all finite. So at some point, one person can only consume so many fish or other protein-based foods before they go bad.

The more we consume the Earth's resources, the farther away we move from living sustainably. The problem with this is that when we live sustainably, our children and their children can enjoy what we have (or even better). So it also helps to ensure a future for future humans.

3. SUSTAINABLE LIVING — HOW DO WE DO IT?

Start simple! You don't have to go out and buy a bunch of stuff to start living sustainably. Just find simple ways to reduce your carbon footprint and use less of the Earth's resources.

One way to do this is by opening a compost pile. Not only will you have your source of fertiliser, but you'll also be contributing to the food chain while cutting back on how much trash you throw away.

Another way you can live sustainably is to start growing your food. Not only will this decrease your food budget, but it will also give you the chance to know where the food that you eat is coming from and how healthy it is.

To live sustainably also means using less water, less energy and fewer resources than you would in a normal lifestyle. For example, this means that instead of having a large house or apartment, you're opting for a smaller space that uses less of your money in utilities.

To live sustainably means that you're using less land, water and labour to produce the things you need.

It means using solar power to heat your home instead of gas. It means growing your food or buying from local farmers instead of big corporations.

And most importantly, living sustainably means thinking about what your legacy to the world will be before it's too late.

It means thinking of your family and taking care of them in the best way possible. And it means making sure that your children have a future to look forward to.

Remember that it's not always about having a lot of money; it's about being happy with what you do have.

You can change your mindset and then change your life!

4. SUSTAINABLE LIVING — TIPS

Here are some tips to get you started:

- *Start a compost pile and use it for fertiliser for your plants.*
- *Grow your food and sell the extras at farmers markets or to friends and family.*
- *Sell the extras at farmers markets or to friends and family. Buy less stuff and use the things you already have.*
- *Buy locally-made goods instead of name-brand items that were made far away.*
- *Buy anti-consumerist goods like food, clothes, and other environmentally friendly goods. These items are clothing made from organic cotton, furniture made from reclaimed materials, or food sourced from local farmers.*
- *Use recyclable materials for crafts to eliminate unnecessary waste.*

5. SUSTAINABLE LIVING — TOOLS / RESOURCES

I like the Low-Cost Living site because they have a great list of tips, resources and tools to get you started on living sustainably. Here's a link to their site: http://livinglowcost.com/

6 . SUSTAINABLE LIVING — WHAT DO YOU THINK?

I hope that you found these tips helpful and that you can start living sustainably in your own life! :)

Sustainable Living Green Architecture

Green architecture taking root in a 'green' neighbourhood will one day be commonplace. However, it remains the domain of small-scale housing, with most efforts focused on individual eco-commuter pods.

Large-scale projects largely remain the preserve of developers, building on the green credentials of previous developments.

Building an entire community with sustainable living in mind is a different matter altogether. It can only be accomplished by private citizens who can invest up to millions of pounds to build their vision.

Not so for a project started by two property developers in the outskirts of Colwick. They are turning a derelict field into Britain's first zero-carbon housing estate.

The developers are working on a social and environmental experiment, which may one day be possible for anyone able to afford green homes – whether in a city, suburb or rural village.

The housing estate will be built on the former Brownsover airfield, a site on the edge of Leicester. The developers have provided plans for 112 homes, each with a self-contained living unit.

The homes would offer energy-saving features such as efficient hot-water systems and solar panels for electricity. In addition, the apartments are being built in an eco-friendly way to achieve a high level of sustainable comfort.

The main house and estate cars would be powered by green electricity generated by local wind farms. A specialist contractor is being employed to design the eco-friendly apartments and houses, which are being developed onsite at the airfield.

An eco-friendly housing estate on land reclaimed from derelict and blight will appear as a five-acre field of new homes and landscaped gardens.

The first phase of the eco-housing estate will include a house, two farm buildings and an eco-friendly farm and garden.

Residents are being offered two 36-month leases, during which time they will be allowed to purchase a home at a discounted price.

At the end of the lease period, residents would pay market value for their property on their chosen date.

The current plans forego any requirement for planning permission or electricity connection with the national grid.

The developers have undertaken extensive work on earthwork and drainage to reduce the site's carbon footprint to zero.

This ambitious project is being carried out by one Property company of residential property; developers based in Colwick.

They have built 24 green homes in the area and plan to provide 1,500 homes in brownfield sites across the country over the next 20 years.

This zero-carbon housing project will begin with a house built on the site and a completed eco-garden. The first phase of the project will be completed by late summer 2008.

With an automated water supply, lighting system, and solar panels, the house will cost £350,000, including landscaping costs.

The two farm buildings and living quarters will cost £250,000 to build and should be finished by autumn 2008.

The eco-friendly farm will be completed and landscaped next year with a water supply.

There are currently around 100,000 such apartments and homes built in Britain each year.

The developers want the eco-housing estate to demonstrate the benefits of carbon-neutral housing and sell into overseas markets before any global warming legislation.

For the project to be a success, it is crucial to control the carbon footprint for each house.

Therefore, the developers use natural energy sources as much as possible and gather rainwater for use in each home.

Each home also has solar panels and state-of-the-art water systems that solar panels and wind turbines will charge.

To offset the carbon footprint of building materials, a construction company has made deals with colleges and universities to use their waste products.

This company will also heat the eco-community using natural energy sources.

Natural energy sources go a long way to reducing a building's carbon footprint, as do sustainable systems for hot and cold water, heating and lighting.

The construction company has also partnered with local farmers to use their land as a straw and animal dung source for its eco-house.

The company will use the dung and straw to heat water and make methane gas, which will be used as a renewable energy source. In addition, each house will have its private sewage system, which will use water from the showers and sinks to generate electricity with particular bacteria already used in power stations.

The developer has undertaken extensive work to reduce its carbon footprint to make it carbon-neutral.

The eco-community would be powered by green electricity generated by local wind farms and a biomass plant on site.

The company also plans to use solar panels for electricity, which will depend on local conditions, is fed into a 24-hour centralised generator that will use waste wood or wood coppice.

A biogas plant onsite will produce electricity from the food waste produced in the eco-community.

Residents will participate in an 'energy efficiency competition', which would involve setting targets that cut overheads and reduce carbon emissions.

The prize would be a carbon offset, which reduces greenhouse emissions made elsewhere – possibly overseas.

The standards involved would be measured in kilowatt-hours per person per year.

The monthly savings required amount to more than a third of the average household energy bill.

To complete the development, the construction company has acquired the land, and it is hoped that an electricity supply can be provided without significant investment.

However, if the grid could not be used, a hydrogen gas-powered electricity plant already in operation will provide energy for each house.

The eco-housing estate would be powered by green energy sources with three wind turbines and a local biomass plant. The developers are currently discussing building a new biomass facility that uses excess heat to create energy for nearby homes.

A short documentary about this project can be seen at *http://www.youtube.com/watch?v=jKf_gDR Q2Ys*

http://www.martonresidentsactiongroup.co. uk/2009/04/14/the-marton-model-for-zero-carbon-housing/

Brian Robarts and Paul Rowlinson try to save rare marshland, BBC News, (23 November 2007)

http://news.bbc.co.uk/1/hi/england/leicesters hire/7043227.stm

East Midlands Today, http://www.youtube.com/watch?v=rsv4wKj QrgU&feature=related

http://www.marketingmag.co.uk/industry-news/sustainability/sustainable-housing-for-boroughs-to-go-ahead–12257422/

http://www.theecologist.org/green_green_liv ing/biodiversity/252389/how_a_q.

http://www.wilsonlab.com/biodiversity/ journal/2003_12_01/065xd9fb8-a7b5-4dd3-a963-5c5f74637a87

SUSTAINABLE LIVING — LINKS

Here are some other great sites that talk about sustainable living:

http://www.dirtguidebooks. com/Sustainable-Living.html

http://naturalnewsblog.com/tag/sustainable-living

http://www.frugallivingnw.com/home-garden/ecofriendly-tips.html

http://www.saveonenergy.com/Home_Impro vement_Diy_Projects_Ecoliving/

http://www.befrugallivebetter.com/ecoliving
.htm

http://www.epa.gov/greenpower/

http://www.ecologyvancouver.com/blog

I hope this book has been helpful to you. We have covered various topics concerning storage container home.

Good luck with your journey!

Thank you for taking the time to read this introductory book. If you found it helpful, then please give us the thumbs-up. Your feedback is most important to us.

You may be interested in other books by this author on the next page.

About The Author

Stirling De Cruz-Coleridge is a published author in many genres. In addition, he's a philanthropist, entrepreneur and a chicken keeper!

Stirling is also a researcher and entrepreneur with over 15 years of experience as a businessman and a keen golf player.

You may be interested in other books by this author; see the next page.

Other Books by Stirling De Cruz-Coleridge

- *Chicken Coop & Run Chicken Keeping*

  For Beginners, Simple Guide To Raising Poultry Flock In Your Backyard.

- *How To Raise Backyard Chickens For Eggs And Meat Or, Keeping Poultry As Pets Discover 10 Quick Tips On Raising Hens And 20 Fun Facts About Chickens*

- *Live Your Life with Success, Good Habits and Love: 45 Highly Effective Habits of Successful People.*

- *Success, Happiness, Power, and Money: How to Make Your Life Awesome in 15 Ways.*

- *Emotional Healing & Personal Transformation: 7 Ways on How to Handle a Breakup When You Still Love Them.*

- *Powerful, Motivational Success Habits and Personal Transformation: 10 Effective Ways to Create Self Confidence and an Awesome Life.*

- *Learning and Memory: How to Use Advanced Strategies & Techniques to Remember More, Learn More, Accelerate Your Brain Power & How to Avoid Memory Deficit in Later Life.*

146

- *Menopausal Brain Fog Memory: Strategies to Help Women Think Straight and Cope Better in the Workplace.*

- *Dating For Men And Women: Essential, Proven Advice, Trustworthy Tips On Finding Love: Guidebook On How To Date Successfully (Self-Help Self-Care Personal Transformation)*

- *Alpaca Animals Guidebook: Keeping Alpacas Simple Guide For Beginners*

- *Golf For Money: Earn Income From Golfing: Beginner's Introduction Guide*

- *Coping with Depression & Anxiety: Emotional Healing After a Relationship Breakup (3 Manuscripts in 1)*

- *Life-Changing Affirmations Adult Coloring Gift Book: Amazing Affirmations Coloring Journal Activity Gift Book for Adults Choosing Happy and Living with Gratitude, Purpose & Meaning*

- *Gratitude: What Is Gratefulness? Why Is The Mind-Body Connection So Powerful and How To Practice It: The Mental Physical and Spiritual Connection of Giving Thank*

Stirling's Amazon Author
Page:

https://amzn.to/3rN346A

Made in United States
Troutdale, OR
09/18/2023

12991905R00092